TRAINING MANUAL

FOR EBOOK AND PAPERBACK
KINDLE CREATE PUBLISHING

A Pragmatic Perspective

MADU AUGUSTINE C, Ph.D

ISBN...............

DEDICATION

This book is specially dedicated to my beloved son, OBUMNEKE, Emmanuel- Augustine Jnr.

ACKNOWLEDGEMENT

I am delighted to be amongst those sharing the story of successfully passing through the hurdles of this 'Skill Create' and emancipation training. First, I thank the Lord almighty for granting us the grace and zeal of astuteness and focus without fail. It is my pleasure to see myself tutored and coached by two great scholars in the persons of Dr. Obasi Otuu Oko and the big brother, Oga-patapata for giving me such action imbued drills at the basic and master classes respectively.

May God keep you in good health of mind and body. My success story cannot be complete without extending a special appreciation to my class colleagues especially Dr. Onyekwere Ezirim for lending a hand of support and encouragement. I am indebted to my lovely wife and children for their understanding and love all through the period of my studies. May God bless all of you out there, amen.

CHAPTER ONE

Introduction Preface

March 3rd 2021 was my first day to be exposed to the basic training module on ebook publishing powered by "Write –For-Me" consulting team for Amazon company. The Basic trainer and facilitator, Dr Obasi Oko admonished all participants to show commitment and diligence in the course of the training so as to obtain the maximum benefits at the end. He emphasized on the need for punctuality to the three- day morning and evening sessions of the Basic training program to be fully equipped to publish their books on the Amazon ebook publishing platform. He equally underscored the gains inherent with the acquisition of the skills which include: Self ebook publishing to enrich one's academic prowess and monetary economies through payment of royalties by Amazon, etc.

CHAPTER TWO

Registration of Training Participants

This section featured the introduction of all those participating in the training tagged "LETS MEET YOU". Here trainees supplied bio data consisting of their full names, discipline, writers or authors, readiness with manuscripts for publication and their expectations from the training.

CHAPTER THREE
Class Assessment Quiz

Trainees were quizzed on related subjects to help sharpen their mindset on the core business and target of the training. Some of the questions include:

Qa. State three things the training is and is not about.

The training is not a mere interaction, a show biz and a gaming conference rather, it is mastery class for e-writing and e-publishing of books and other literary articles, a navigation from the conventional 'Analog' to 'Digital' writing world and a platform to creating alternative means of moneymaking through royalties from ebook sales and services.

CHAPTER FOUR

- **S**till on Writing

Qb. What is Writing and Strong Writing?

Writing can be defined as the ability to scribble down anything on a piece of paper or device for purposes of communicating an information while strong writing is an act of composing a text for publication purposes and usually in a more permanent medium than in ordinary writing.

CHAPTER FIVE
Writing Continues

Qc. When is writing said to be effective?

Writing is said to be effective when it communicates the core object intended. In other words, since communication is a two-way thing, we write to receive a feedback, therefore our writings should be such that can be understood and or elicit reactions or feedback. When such is achieved then writing is said to be effective. Effective writing summarily is defined in other words in terms of Systematic Accuracy.

CHAPTER SIX
Writing Continues

Qd. What is purposeful writing?

Purposeful writing simply means a thoughtful ad intentionally motivated write-up, writing that satisfy the domain of

What is being written ie the subject matter?

Who is being written ie the person(s) the writing is meant to address?

Why writing at the particular time?

Which group or class of people is the writing to address? and

How best to communicate so as to achieve the desired effect?

When the write answers these various domains then an effective writing is said to have been achieved.

CHAPTER SEVEN

About Books

Qe. What is a Book?

A book can be defined as a collection or compilation of ideas structured in a sequential manner and bound for convenience and easy perusal.

Qf. What is blurb of book?

Blurb of a book is a brief description of a book in a way that can attract public interest and patronage. A book blurb is usually found at the inside back cover of the book and may be written by the author or publisher or other persons.

CHAPTER EIGHT
Getting to Know Ebook

This chapter brings us to the ice ball of the training. It is therefore expedient to know the meaning of the subject matter of this training "e-book"

Qg. What is the ebook?

An ebook is a short form of electronic book, Books in digital form and accessed via electronic media such as computer, android phones, iPads, etc, Ebooks are published on the internet and can be downloaded and printed as paper books where and when necessary. Having ebook as a technological innovation is one good thing that has happened to the society hence, it is gradually reducing the relevance of paper book. This is true as more than 80% of world population has experienced civilization and embraced modern technology. To this end, reading and writing paper books would soon become a thing of the past making ebooks most relevant and convenient method of writing for all.

CHAPTER NINE
Ebooks and Paper books
- Any Difference?

Qh. What is the difference between Paper book and ebook?

While ebooks are accessed vis digital aids, paper book are accessed offline. Since ebooks are digital in nature, it is possible and easy to carry thousands of such books in a piece of handset or laptop, its production and processing is timely and labour seamless. The reverse of course is the case in the movement of paper books. Paper books are seen everywhere either in hard or paper back covers and quite bulky to handle.

CHAPTER TEN

Origin of Ebooks

Who launched the first ebook and the name given it? What year was it launched?

The first person to launch an ebook was Michael S. Hart and the first ebook is tagged 'Project Gutenberg' when he digitalized the United States declaration of independence. The ebook was then first launched in 1971.

CHAPTER ELEVEN
Masters Ebook Creation
And Publishing

The Masters ebook creation and publishing class was the advanced segment of ebook basic training program. The course is broken into different segments as follows;

i.   Registration and Accreditation.

ii.   Manual formatting of manuscript (Advanced methods),

iii.   Opening of the Kindle Create Account and signing n

iv.   Filling of the required information on Account Registration

v.   Move to the Kindle Create page, click on the bookshelf and manual complete the details extracted from your manuscript which is tored as the Kindle create file

vi.   Click on the Bookshelf to access the Book cover creation section

vii.   Upload your manuscript in readiness to publish then move to the Electronic part of the whole process starting with the KINDLE CREATE APP download.

Ebook Creation and processes continued

viii. Download the App

ix. Call up your work from the Kindle Create file store or CHOOSE from your document (DOC), PDF file in your system and import or upload the kindle create system.

x. Accept to go with the automatic format provided by the system or you reject and manual format your work with the formatting tools provided by the kindle create mechanism

xi. You are done and good to go publishing

CHAPTER THIRTEEN

REGISTRATION AND ACCREDITATION OF PARTICIPANTS

All those who successfully participated in the basic training session and assigned Registration codes are admitted to the Masters class. To this effect, successful participants submitted their choice pictures, payment details, Names and phone numbers of the Basic class teachers and details of expectations from the Masters class.

CHAPTER FOURTEEN

Manual formatting of
manuscript (Adv. methods)

The manual formatting gives the trainee the latitude to custom format his work, in such a manner that is acceptable when uploaded via the KINDLE CREATE medium for instance, manuscripts are either in word DOC, PDF, etc. Formatting in a nut shell is the process of arranging your manuscript to wear the appearance and features you will like the viewing readers and public appreciate it. This is entirely your choice to make but you are to work by the rules of the kindle create app to avoid your work being rejected. To this therefore, you are to ensure a level of orderliness in performing tasks like choice of fonts, choice of size of the book to be Kindle create compliant and other formatting actions. This manual preparation of the manuscript when properly done makes your publishing task an easy one. However, where you are not prepared for all those, the kindle create app provides you with a formatting tool to choose from and settle with your choice.

CHAPTER FIFTEEN

Understanding the KDP Configuration

KDP allows you self- publish ebooks and paperbacks for free. There is however some category of materials that KDP does not accept for publication and they include, magazines, periodicals etc because the system was not configured for such items. Publishing with KDP gives you full rights to your book

CHAPTER SIXTEEN OPENING OF
THE KINDLE CREATE ACCOUNT

Here, the process requires the publisher to sign up and sign in to the Amazon Kindle Direct Publishing (KDP) Account by taking the following steps

Step 1. Go to either Google, Chrome, etc search engines.

Step 2. Type http//Kdp.amazon.com

Step 3. Sign-up if a first time user otherwise sign-in if an existing account holder

CHAPTER SEVENTEEN
The kindle Create Page

Once you sign in, you are assigned the Account ID which appears on the down part of the left side while the KDP form props upon the right The form is in three parts of Personal Information, Getting Paid and Tax Information. Properly fill them and not to worry about filling the getting paid section due to some unresolved issues, choose the option of receiving your pay through cheques and move to the Tax payment section and fill the form but at any point you have a problem and there is an (i) meaning information, you click on it for possible options. When completed and submitted, your tax information submission gets approval. You then save and click finished and return to the main page. It is vital to properly fill the Tax Information since it is a prerequisite for accessing the Authorship and Publishing page of the KDP.

CHAPTER EIGHTEEN FILLING OF THE AUTHOR/PUBLISHER FORM

Once, approval is given on your tax information then you are good to go with the next line of action on Kindle Create Publishing. Once more *It's important to note that you need to complete your tax information BEFORE you can publish your first book. So don't skip this step*

This page expects, you supply required information about you and your manuscript hence the following sequence of information is needed.

- Crafting Your Book Title & Subtitle
- Writing Your Book Description
- Choosing the Right Keywords
- Selecting the Right Categories
- Uploading Your Manuscript
- Creating a Book Cover
- Creating your paper back

CHAPTER NINETEEN

Book Description

A description is essentially a short written narrative that illustrates what your book is about. It should be written like a sales page to capture the interest of your reader. Readers usually look out for the title, cover and book description as major areas of captivation to draw them close to the book. Therefore, you must not lose sight of this. Here are some strategies to help craft your perfect description:

- Make your first sentence as enticing as possible
- Write your description like a sales page or advertisement, not a dry summary of your book
- Have the description feel personal and empathetic
- Detail the benefits your reader will gain by reading your book

CHAPTER TWENTY

Choice of Right Keywords and selection of the Right Categories

Keywords are specific words or phrases used to describe your book. If someone was looking for a book on your topic, they might type one of those keywords into Amazon or Google in order to find it. A typical example of keywords especially if your book is about perseverance, you might find keywords like this useful:

- how to have perseverance
- what is perseverance

- perseverance examples
- persevering
- persevering when it's hard

CHAPTER TWENTY- ONE

Here are a few tips when publishing on Amazon in order to rank in more categories:

- Research your competitors' keywords
- Choose trending categories with lower competition
- Acquire additional categories by contacting Amazon and asking for keyword placement.

CHAPTER TWENTY-TWO
Uploading DOC, PDF etc file

Here's how to upload your book to Amazon:

- In your Kindle Direct Publishing account, go to "Your Bookshelf".
- Locate and click on "Kindle eBook Actions" next to the title of your book.
- Locate and click on "Edit eBook Content".
- Click on "Upload eBook manuscript".
- Upload your manuscript file on your computer.
- Upload complete!

Once Amazon finishes uploading your file, a confirmation message will be sent and you can preview the uploaded file to check for any errors. You can upload the manuscript as many times as you want and the new version will override the existing. It's important to check how your book looks using the "Look Inside" feature once the book is live on Amazon.

CHAPTER TWENTY-THREE
Create Your Book Cover

When it comes to publishing a successful book on Amazon, having a perfect book cover design is one of the most important aspects to get right. Contrary to what we were told growing up, people *do*, in fact, judge a book by its cover. It's actually one of the biggest deterrents. Your cover is exactly how your book will be judged at first glance.

Make sure that your cover is created professionally and that it will stand apart from the rest of the books in you genre or category in places like

- 100 Covers

- 99 Designs
- Happy Self-Publishing

Prices will depend on the level of service, but these sites will give you plenty of amazing graphic designers to choose from! It's a great investment that will make your book stand out perfectly.

Madu Augustine Chinwe Yadirichukwu hails from Ibiasoegbe in Oru West LGA of Imo State, Nigeria. Austine went through ticks and thin in pursuit of greener pastures. As a small boy, Austin had nurtured a dream to ascend the brink of academic excellence and today, he holds the prestigious Intermediate (Affiliate) certificate of the Chartered Institute of Purchasing and Supply (CIPS) London and thereafter obtained the final professional certificate and Diploma of the Chartered Institute of Purchasing and Supply Management of Nigeria (CIPSMN), Holder of the great Ife Advanced Diploma Certificate in Purchasing and Supply, Masters in Business Administration (MBA) degree from University of Calabar (UNICAL), Master of Science(MSC) Degree in Economics from Enugu State University of Science and Technology (ESUT)and Doctor of Philosophy (Ph.D) Degree in Economics from University of Calabar

He is a member of very distinguished professional bodies among which are, Affiliate, Chartered Institute of Purchasing & Supply (ACIPS) London, Member, Chartered Institute of Purchasing & Supply Management of Nigeria (MCIPSN), A fellow of the Chartered Instotute of Public Diplomacy and Management (CIPDM), Fellow, Occupational Safety and Health Associaton (OSHA) UK. Nigeria Region

ABOUT THE AUTHOR

Dr. Madu Augustine, Jp

ABOUT THE AUTHOR

Madu Augustine Chinwe Yadirichukwu hails from Ibiasoegbe in Oru West LGA of Imo State, Nigeria. Austine went through ticks and thin in pursuit of greener pastures. As a small boy, Austin had nurtured a dream to ascend the brink of academic excellence and today, he holds the prestigious Intermediate (Affiliate) certificate of the Chartered Institute of Purchasing and Supply (CIPS) London and thereafter obtained the final professional certificate and Diploma of the Chartered Institute of Purchasing and Supply Management of Nigeria (CIPSMN), Holder of the great Ife Advanced Diploma Certificate in Purchasing and Supply, Masters in Business Administration (MBA) degree from University of Calabar (UNICAL), Master of Science(MSC) Degree in Economics from Enugu State University of Science and Technology (ESUT)and Doctor of Philosophy (Ph.D) Degree in Economics from University of Calabar.

He is a member of very distinguished professional bodies among which are, Affiliate, Chartered Institute of Purchasing & Supply (ACIPS) London, Member, Chartered Institute of Purchasing & Supply Management of Nigeria (MCIPSN), Associate Member Nigerian Institute of Management (ANIM,), Member Nigerian Institute of Entrepreneurship (MNIOE), Fellow, Chartered Institute of Public Diplomacy and Management (FCIPDM) ,Fellow, Occupational Safety and Health Association (OSHA) UK, Nigeria Region. Austin as fondly called by admirers, was one time Imo State Secretary of CIPSMN 2003 -2005, Chairman, CIPSMN 2005 – 2008, South-East Zonal Coordinator and member of council of CIPSMN, 2008-2012. A scholarly fellow, Dr. Madu has a textbook titled "Purchasing Practice and Techniques in Q & A form Plus International Purchasing" (An Abridged Text), five Journal Publications and five conference/ workshop papers to his credit.

A registered Consultant, Chief Executive, aUSTINO cONSULTS, Nig., He has successfully served as a resource person at several Conferences including the ones organized by the Chartered Institute of Purchasing Supply Management of Nigeria. He had also tutored several students, civil and public servants in their quest for professional qualifications and CIPSMN's certification among these today are Directors of Procurement in the various Ministries and Parastatals across Nigeria. Dr. A C Madu JP grew in ranks to become a Chief Purchasing Officer in the Federal Polytechnic Nekede and later held many appointed positions as follows; Pioneer HOD, Internally Generated Revenue(iGR) Federal Polytechnic Nekede, Owerri, 2010 -2012, Deputy Director (IGR) 2012- 2014, HOD (Accounts) TEDC, FPNO, 2014 -2015, HOD, Mgt. Accounts, FPNO 2015 -2017 and later Senior Lecturer by conversion and a Principal Lecturer

He became Head of Department, Purchasing and Supply between 2019 and 2020. He headed several committees in the Institution with prominence to Choir/Music Subcommittee of the schools Matriculation and Convocation Ceremonies from 1985 to date and as a gifted singer and composer, Dr Madu single handedly composed and conducts the today's FPNO's celebrated Matriculation Anthem titled "On the plains of Nekede" and also modified the ever 'green' and melodious Polytechnic song titled "Nestling on the Nekede Plains".
He is happily married to Mrs. Henrietha Ngozi Madu and blessed with precious children.